The Great Light In Masonry

A Little Book in praise of the Book of Books

Joseph Fort Newton

The Temple Publishers
http://TheTempleBooks.com

Copyright 2003
The Temple Publishers
ISBN 0-9724445-3-X

THE INNER GUARD

A LITTLE book made up of words spoken and written at various times in honor of the Holy Bible, celebrating its spiritual faith, its moral majesty, its literary wonder, and above all its revelation of the will of God for the life of man.

Our Craft is wise in making the noblest book on earth its Guide, Prophet, and Friend, uniting the light of Revelation and the Law of Nature in the service of the Brotherly Life.

Far better than any words about the Bible are the words of the Bible itself, to read which is to know whence we came, why we are here, and the direction and destiny of our days.

-J. F. N.

THE GREAT LIGHT IN MASONRY

CHAPTER I
THE MASTER BOOK

TIME is a river and books are boats. Many volumes have started down the stream of years only to be wrecked and buried forever in its sands. Few indeed are the books that live out a single century. Here, as in all else, the law of the survival of the fittest applies, and there is no critic so terrible as Time. No book lives save as it tells of that in the life of man which grows not old and fades not away. Homer lives not simply for his art, but for his story of great adventure, his pictures of man and woman, of love and joy and death in the days when life was new. Virgil lives not only because he fashioned some of the noblest lines ever molded by mortal lips, but because he sings of the wayfaring of the soul in a far-off, unreturning past. Human things, not less than Divine things, never die.

Our Bible is not a Book, but a Divine Library, as St. Jerome called it so long ago. It is not the record of one mind or of one age, but of many minds covering a long stretch of time–the history of the life of a people having a genius for religion as the Greeks had a genius for art and philosophy, and as the Romans had a genius for jurisprudence. Other nations had sacred books as a part of their literatures, but the literature of the Hebrews was wholly religious. The ruling trait of that race was its sense of the Unseen, its vision of the moral Jaw, its passion for God. Here was a folk whose government was a theocracy, and whose patriotism was piety. Their poetry kindled its flame at the altar of faith. Their architecture was a House of Prayer. The Muse of their History was the Spirit of Holiness. Surely it is not a thing strange that the poets of such a people became prophets, their faces aglow with moral idealism, their lips speaking words of fire. Nor is it a matter of wonder that the most religious race in all history should have written the sacred book of mankind, the moral classic of the world.

One may say, reverently, that the life of Jesus, so far as we can understand it, was the consummate flower of the piteous, passionate, aspiring life of that mighty race-just as Plato was the crowning glory of a race of thinkers. On His human side Jesus was surely the focus, the glowpoint, at which the God-inspired soul of His people, melted by sorrow and purified by fire, became incandescent with heavenly light. It was as if the scattered atoms of an old chaos had at last been gathered into a planet yea, a Sun to light our dark world; as if the wandering tones of many harps had found a home in the bosom of one sovereign Harmony. This does not account for Christ, but it does help us to mark the path by which He came and the tradition in which He stood. It is only to say that God appeared to a race that had eyes to see, and spoke to men who had ears to hear.

The land of the Bible is an enduring commentary on a 'Book which has in it the rugged grandeur of a work of nature. It is a tiny land, shut in on two sides by deserts, and on the other sides by mountain and sea; a rough and broken land where shaggy, thunder-split hills enclose narrow valley, and beauty sits on the brow of barrenness; of mutable climate and varying moods; lorded over by blazing suns and deep lucid nights; a land ever in extremes-now dried up as in a furnace, now flooded with loud waters. An isolated land, with the Dead Sea at the south and snowy mountains at the north, yet it was a highway of trade and the battlefield of rival empires, its history a long-drawn tragedy of war and pillage and sorrow. The Bible is a mirror of its motherland, alike of its history and its scenery, where suns rise in beauty and set in splendor, and rivers flow, and flowers bloom, and lightnings rush like angry painters across the sky. As Emerson said:

> "Out from the heart of nature rolled
> The burdens of the Bible old;
> The litanies of nations came,
> Like the volcano's tongue of flame,
> Up from the burning "ore below-
> The canticles of love and woe."

Open the Bible where you will, and the first impression is that of vastness. It has in it the curve of the earth and the arch of the sky. Great and wide like' the world, it is rooted in the abyss of creation and rises into the blue mysteries of heaven. There are continents of truth, seas of mystery, rivers flowing from invisible springs, valleys rich with harvest, marshes of melancholy, depths sombre and sunless, and mountains that pierce the clouds. It is a world of reality and fact, a world in which men live and love, and sin and suffer, and hope and die, in the sight of the sun. It is the world as God made it, and is making it, with Divine power in His forces, Divine order in its ongoings, and Divine purpose in its end. The book has four characters in it, God and Man, the sky and the dirt. It has in it the strength and massive grandeur of elemental things, and no one can read it aright without feeling that he is in the presence of the big, eternal meanings of life.

The Bible is not a book of philosophy. It does not argue. It is a book of Vision whose story moves between two mighty seers–Moses, whose vision brooded over the dark chaos of old, whence order and beauty emerged, and St. John, whose insight forecast in solemn apocalypse the final issue of man and the world. What a history it recites! It begins at the beginning, with the wandering shepherds and wayfarers in the dim morning of time. We see the rise of the home and the family, of the tribe and the nation; a race passing through slavery into the vestibule of civilized life; the gradual building of a rich and complex social order; its prosperity, its splendor, its testing time, and its final fall, "because it knew not the time of its visitation." The story begins in a Garden and ends in the coming of the City of God, where there is no sadness nor weeping, and the whole is set against a majestic background of eternity-birth and death, promise and fulfilment, victory and defeat, all the drama of humanity in the presence of God.

As one reads there comes a shock of surprise that the essentials of human nature, its joys and woes and upward-leaping hopes, remain seemingly unaltered by all the vicissitudes of time and change. Across the rise and fall of nations, over the feverish life of groping generations long since vanished, there sounds the unchanging music of faith and hope, of love and loss and longing. In a remote story of a Moabite girl- a page let fall from an old picture of life, as if by accident-men and women find to-day the one perfect expression of undying affection: "Where thou goest I will go; and where thou lodgest I will lodge; thy people shall be my people, thy God my God. Where thou diest I will die, and there will I be buried; the Lord do so to me and more also, if aught but death, part me from thee." In a record of fierce tribal war, amidst scenes of cunning and barbaric vengeance, we hear the most musical of all laments of friendship – the living for the dead: "I am distressed for thee, my brother Jonathan; very pleasant hast thou been to me; thy love for me was wonderful, passing the love of woman." An undated drama of the desert, full of its wide spaces and awful questionings—a book mysterious and magnificent which has drawn the deepest minds to its study—gives voice to a plaintive cry which not time nor fortune has modified: "As the waters fail from the sea, and the flood decayeth and drieth up; so man lieth down and riseth not; till the heavens be no more; they shall not wake, nor be raised out of their sleep."

Here, in this splendid spacious Book, one finds every variety of thought and mood and feeling, from a biting skepticism to a death-defying faith, from a sob of despair to a shout of ecstasy. It contains passages of the boldest denial—impeachments of the beneficence of God more fierce than any in the choruses of Swinburne—and an agnosticism more ultimate than even that of Omar the Tentmaker, without his scent and sheen of the flesh. A bit of sensuous love poetry is set side by side with the most bitter and shattering pessimism, crying like the wail of chill winds in a deserted city. Here are prayers that have wings, and songs of the victory of faith over death and time; confessions that lay bare the soul of man; pilgrim hymns; elegies portraying the majesty of God and the fleetingness of man; prophecies that flash the future in their mirrors. On the music marches until, at last, there breaks into it the sweetest voice that man has ever heard, whose words are the truth about life, and whose tones evoke melodies that echo forever.

At sundry times and in divers manners this music is heard, like a great organ with myriad keys on which a Master plays. In the Bible there is almost every form of literary art—history, poetry, drama, fiction, biography, letters, lyrics, elegies, epics, epigrams, proverbs, parables, allegories, and the dreams of apocalyptic seers. John was a mystic, Ezekiel a divine dreamer, David a lyric poet, and Solomon a kind of Bible Benjamin Franklin. Each has his own imagery and thought, his own tone and style, but the whole is united by one spirit, one passion, one hunger for eternity. As men come to know the laws of great literature, how it grows and how it is interpreted, the variety and sublimity of the Bible will be unveiled. They will hush their debates and listen to its far-sounding, Divine cadences, many-toned and melting, knowing that a Book which grew out of a profound morality and a lofty spiritual life, if rightly used and obeyed, will produce in us, 'infallibly, the kind of life which produced it. They will know that it is inspired because it inspires them, revealing heights and depths unguessed before-heights where the Infinite woos the finite into its mystery, and the depths, where men find the heart of the world. It was not a Christian scholar, but a skeptic famous for his stinging wit—Heine, whose poetry is a blended smile, tear and sneer-who wrote these words:

"What a Book! Stranger still than its contents is for me its style, in which every word is, so to speak, a product of nature, like a tree, a flower, like the sea, the stars, like man himself. One does not know how, one does not know why, one finds it altogether quite natural. In Homer, the other great book, the style is a product of art, and the material always, as in the Bible, is taken from reality, yet it shapes itself into a poetic form as though recast in the melting pot of the human spirit. In the Bible there is not the least trace of art; it is the style of a memorandum book in which the Absolute Spirit entered the daily incident with the same actual truthfulness with which we write our washing list."

Some have denied that the Bible is an unveiling of the Divine nature, but no one doubts that it is a revelation of human nature. Here is a book that knows man, the road whence he came and what is in his heart. It finds us, as Coleridge said, strips us to the soul, and makes us see as in a mirror what manner of men we really are. No other book is so candid with us, so honest, so stern, so tender, so mercilessly merciful in its searchings of the strange soul within us. No man can stand before it and have any vanity left in him. It knows our innermpst, secret sin—the lust that defiles, the passion that. sears, the envy that gnaws, the pride that is foolishness. Righteousness is its one great word—righteousness in God demanding righteousness in man. It teaches, as does all great tragedy from Euripides to Shakespeare, the iron law of destiny—the sowing and reaping of sin. But in the Bible this law is suffused with a vast tenderness, as if to show that it is a law of love. The moral earnestness of this Book makes one tremble, as its ineffable pity makes one weep. No other book has in it such a blend of charity and rebuke. The mercy of God is in it and He remembers that we are dust — hence its voice of many thunders and its whisper as of a mother over her child.

In other hooks we see humanity struggling upward, building a Tower of Babel; in the Bible we feel that something comes down to man, as at Pentecost. It moves under a whispering sky. All who read it know that our human life is from above downward, and that our help is from God. Other books have rafters and a roof. The Bible has none. In Shakespeare the unseen world appears in weird ghosts or flitting witches, as a thing uncanny and dreadful. Not so in the Bible. The subtle air of eternity blows through it, like the sweet winds that wander over the meadows. It talks of the eternal world with a simple artless faith, as a child talks of the stars, as if heaven were as real as is earth, and as natural. It makes us know that God is here, that eternity is now, that life has ageless fellowships—that every truth is full of Divine mystery, and every day charged with unknown, immortal meanings. Hence there is a power in this master Book not found in any other—a power of faith, a sense of unseen reality, which makes men broad of mind and tall of soul. Look into the life of Gladstone, with his fine moral idealism, or into the life of Lincoln, with his cool sanity and his stern but delicate justice, and you will learn that they drew much of their strength from the Bible. It is no wonder that the prophetic eloquence of Lincoln echoes with Bible music, as do so many great passages of our literature-like that noble page in the "*School of Saints*," like that forest scene in "*Westward Ho!,*" like that unforgettable refrain in Thackeray when Henry Esmond returns from the wars. Oh, let us take this wise old Book to our hearts, and not only love it but live with it, making it the prophet of our inner life, lest the faith that makes us men be crushed by the tramp of heavy years. If we use it wisely, we may commune with those in whom God dwelt, even as He dwells in us, albeit we do not yet know Him whom to know aright is life eternal.

All men feel, at times, an oppressive sense of human insignificance. Millions of men lived here upon this earth before us, and have vanished. We do not know their names. Like us, they were pilgrims and had to pass on. Soon we must follow along the same beaten path into the common oblivion, and our footsteps will be trodden out by the oncoming multitudes. It is in the midst of meditations such as these that the dear old Bible brings us its sweetest message. It fills us with a sense of the dignity of the human personality, its sacredness, and its august destiny. It tells us that our little lives, brief, broken and frail as they are, have a meaning for God; that death is not the end of all, but that beyond its shadow there hovers and waits a larger life. It makes life worth while and opens gates of wonder. God be thanked for a Book which knows so much of the weakness of man, his wickedness and his waywardness, and yet holds up so high an ideal and so grand a hope.

But there is something else in the Bible—a quality so delicate, so elusive, and yet so strong, which no words may ever hope to capture or define. We call is spirituality, a hallowing spirit, an indwelling presence, which gives to this book a nameless and ineffable power and charm. We know what is; we feel it; it rises from the page like a perfume—but no one can put it into words. Religion is a Divine life, not a Divine science, and life cannot be turned into a book. The worth of the Bible is the witness it bears to the reality of God, its testimony that He is found of those who seek Him, and that he lives in the souls of men. As such it is a symbol of a Book greater than itself 'the volume of the Faith of Man, the Book of the Will of God as humanity has learned it in the midst of the years-which Lowell had in mind when he wrote:

"Slowly the Bible of the race is writ,
　　And not on paper leaves nor leaves of stone;
Each age, each kindred, adds a verse to it,
　　Texts of despair or hope, of joy or moan.
While swings the sea, while mists the mountains shroud,
　　While thunder's surges burst on cliffs of cloud,
Still at the prophet's feet the nations sit."

Books are transient and will pass away. Homer, Sophocles, Dante, Shakespeare, and the Bible itself, are all doomed. When time is done they are done. But the life of God in the soul of man can never die. It will live when the globe itself, and all which it inherits, shall dissolve like a dream and leave not a rack behind. Of that, eternal life the Bible bears witness in words the simplest, the deepest, the sanest, the truest and the sweetest that man has heard ,in his long journey, and it is therefore that we love it.

CHAPTER II
THE SUPREMACY OF THE BIBLE

My subject takes it to be a fact that the Bible is the one supreme book of the world. And so it is. Argument is unnecessary; the fact proves it. No one denies it who has any regard at all either for the witness of history or for the realities of life. As Seeley said, the greatest work of individual literary genius shows by the side of the Bible like some building of human hands beside the peak of Teneriffe. With this let us join the words of Scherer, written out of the depths of his skepticism, "If there is anything certain in the world it is that the destiny of the Bible is linked with the destiny of holiness on earth." Not only was the Bible the loom on which our own language was woven, but it has a place equally in the history and the heart of mankind which no other book may ever hope to have.

Even those who have assailed the Bible have seldom, if ever, assailed the book itself, but nearly always some dogma about the Bible. By the same token, those who defend the Bible more often defend some theory about it, forgetting that the fate of the Bible is not bound up with the fortunes of any dogma as to its origin, infallibility, or authority. There is no need that anyone defend the Bible. It is the Bible that defends us from the besieging vanities of life, from the rude cynicism of the world, from the lusts of flesh and the fear of the grave. What men need to do is to be still and listen to its great and simple words, telling the story of God and the Soul and their eternal life together; and whoso does that will know what poor Heine meant when he wrote these words from what he called his mattress grave:

"I attribute my enlightenment entirely and simply to the reading of a book. Of a book! Yes, and it is an old honest book, modest.. as nature, modest as the sun which warms us, as the bread which nourishes us, a book as full of love and blessing as the old mother who reads it with her dear, trembling lips; and this book is the Bible. With right it is named the Holy Scriptures. He who has lost his God can find Him again in this book; and he who has never known Him is here struck by the breath of the Divine Word."

Because this is so, because the Bible is so much wiser than its defenders, what is here said of its unique supremacy is by way of illustration, not in proof of my thesis.. If we contrast the Bible with other venerated writings, we find that it stands alone and apart, very unlike the Upanishads, the Zend-Avesta and the Koran, not only because it is so much more practical, so much less speculative, so rich and varied in its music; but because it shows us, more clearly than any other, the growth of man in his knowledge of God, of himself, of good and evil, of law and love and truth. In fact, it is a Book of Life, not a mere record of intellectual speculation about life, and as a man reads it he sees, as in a mirror, the history of his own soul. Moreover, it comes to us from a time when man saw the big meanings of life with a freshness of insight, a directness, unobscured by passage through media that blur and confuse, without learned subtleties and those ingenious concealments which rob us of reality.

Written before life was "sicklied o'er with the pale cast of thought," it has a vividness, a vitality, a sanity, an artless simplicity, and a lucidity as of the morning light, not to be found anywhere else.

Thirty years ago a great savant characterized the Bible as a collection of the rude imaginings of Syria, the worn-out bottle of Judaism into which the generous new wine of science was being poured. No doubt he was angry when he said so, else he would not have said a thing so foolish. Whereupon the noblest literary critic of our day stated once for all the reason why, from the point of view of literature alone, the Bible lives and will live when we and all those now upon the earth have fallen into dust. He said:

"The new wine of science is a generous vintage, undoubtedly, and deserves all the respect it gets from us; so do those who make it and serve it out; they have so much intelligence; they are so honest and fearless. But whatever may become of their new wine in a few years when the wine-dealers shall have passed away, when the savant is forgotten as any star-gazer of Chaldea—the "old bottle' is going to be older yet—the Bible is going' to be eternal. Coming from the heart of man it goes straight to the heart This is the kind of literature that never does die; a fact which the. world has discovered long ago."

Here the point is that, as a record of human life in the gray years of old, and apart from its divine revelation, the Bible belongs to the things immortal, and will live while human nature is the same. Consider for a moment this fact, established as it is by the terrible testing of time, and you will see why all attacks on the Bible fail, and why any defense of it is unnecessary. Our great critic—it is Watts-Dunton, if you would know his name— proceeds to discuss the style of the Bible, which he calls the "great style," more easily recognized than defined, but which he ventures to define as unconscious power blended with unconscious grace. This style, so august in its simplicity and truthfulness, allows a writer to touch upon any subject with no risk of defilement, because it tells the thing as it is with a clarity which leaves no suggestion of evil. Also, whensoever this style is attained, it moves with the rhythm of life itself, lifting us into a realm where a thousand years are as a day, and where a whisper echoes forever. That is why the heart cry of an exile in old Babylon, or an echo of an hour of prayer in the hills of Judea, lives and speaks to the heart of man to-day, as if time were a fiction. As we may read:

"Now the great features of Bible rhythm are a recognized music apart from a recognized law-'artifice' so completely abandoned that we forget we are in the realm of art—pauses so divinely set that they seem to be 'wood-notes wild'—though all the while they are, and must be, governed by a mysterious law too subtly sweet to be formulated; and all kinds of beauties infinitely beyond the triumphs of the metricist, but beauties that are unexpected. There is a metre, to be sure, but it is that of the 'moving music which is life'; it is the living metre of the surging 'sea within the soul of him who speaks. And if this is so in other parts of the Bible, what is it in the Psalms, where the "flaming steeds of song, though really kept strongly in hand, seem to run reinless as the wild horses of the wind!"

II

Let me illustrate a little, if only to show how high the simplest words of the Bible tower above the loftiest peaks of poetry, as the Alps out-top the masonry of man. Take the eulogy of man which Shakespeare puts into the mouth of Ham-, let, and which has been called the point where the master poet raised prose to the sublimest pitch of verse. The words are familiar:

"That goodly frame, the earth, seems to me a sterile promontory; this most excellent canopy, the air, look you, this brave o'erhanging firmament, this majestical roof fretted with golden fire, it appears no other thing to me than a foul and pestilent congregation of vapors. What a piece of work is man! how noble in reason! how infinite in faculty; in form and moving how express and admirable; in action how like an angel; in apprehension how like a god; the beauty of the world; the paragon of animals."

There is the rich and fluent style of the spacious days of Elizabeth—ornate, apostrophic, brilliant. Here is wonder indeed, albeit not that "wise wonder" in front of a universe now luminous and lovely, now dark and terrible, of which our critic speaks. Nor do we find here that noble humility before Him in whose great hand we stand. How much deeper and truer, how much more faithful to reality are these lines from the Eighth Psalm on exactly the same theme; how noble they are in their stripped simplicity, how chaste and moving their music, touched with that haunting pathos which one hears in all Bible melody:

"When I consider Thy heavens, the work of Thy fingers, the moon and the stars which Thou hast ordained, what is man, th"at Thou are mindful of him? and the son of man, that Thou visitest him? Thou hast made him but a little lower than the angels, and hast crowned him with glory and honor. Thou hast made him to have dominion over the works of Thy hands; Thou hast put all things under his feet; all sheep and oxen, yea, and the beasts of the field; the fowls of the air, and the fish of the sea, and whatsoever passeth through the paths of the seas."

Surely it is something more than old association which makes the sundering difference between these two passages. How tawdry and highflown the one seems alongside the grave and simple truthfulness of the other; how world far they are apart in their attitude toward the life of man and his place in the order of the world. Both celebrate the dignity of man, but in what different ways, against what different backgrounds; one under a roof fretted with golden fire, the other: under a sky that has no roof nor rafter; one as if man were a kind of god exiled on a sterile promontory, the other full of wonder that God is even mindful of a being so fragile and fleeting. The difference is fundamental, and it justifies the saying of Newman that in the Bible, and most of all in the Gospels, there is a manifestation of the divine so special as to make it appear, from the contrast, as if nothing were known of God where the Bible is unknown. Of course this is not true, for God has not left Himself without witnesses in any land or age; but if anyone would feel the full force of the fact, let him take any book known to man, even the greatest, and read it alongside the Bible.

Of the influence of the Bible on civilization much has been written, but the story has never and can never be told. Even as far back as the days of Chrysostom, the Bible could be read in languages Syrian, Indian, Persian, Armenian, Scythian and Samaritan. Now it can be read in almost every tongue under heaven, and the fact that it is the one book that can be universally translated is a touching proof that God is not far from any tribe, and that in the lowest human being His image shines. Poor raiment for His word many of these dialects are, but somehow that mighty book can clothe itself in each. One version, however, and that infinitely slower and more difficult to make, remains to be achieved, and that is the translation of the Bible into the life of humanity. When that translation is finished, as it will be at last, there will be a new heaven and a new earth wherein dwelleth righteousness and the peace of God.

III

And this brings us to the central and grand fact about the Bible, by which it is set apart from all other books whatsoever, and which invests it with an ineffable power and beauty: it is the Book of the Presence of God. Wherever the Bible goes it brings a sense of the presence of God. Its first truth is God, its last truth is God, the basis of its uprising passion and prophecy, the keynote of its far-sounding melody, is the reality of God, whose presence is the splendor of the world, and whose awful will the sun and stars obey. When He is known to be near, all things are transfigured; when He is felt to be far away, its music becomes a cry in the night. It does not argue about God; it reveals Him, and the romance of its story is: the unfolding of His life in the tangled and turbulent life of man. Hence the progress of faith portrayed in the Bible; but in the struggle and conflict of all those groping generations the ;, living God abides, and man walks in the midst of revelations.

If we inquire in what way God makes Himself known to man in the Bible, we ask the profoundest question in the entire range of religious interests: Does the eternal God speak to man? If so, how? No one may answer such questions, except to say that truth may be regarded either as the gift of God or as the achievement of man, because it is both. Every truth is, from the divine side, revelation, and from the human, discovery. Jacob wrestling with the angel in the dawn is the eternal parable of revelation. For, if truth is a gift it is also a trophy, since even the divine reason is unable to disclose His truth to man until, by virtue of his growth of soul, man is ready and worthy and willing to receive it. Thus, every truth that God gives man wins, and every truth that man wins from the mystery of life God bestows. Since God and man are interwoven in the finding of truth, collaborators, so to speak, in the process of revelation, how can man know when the thought of God is made known to him? Here is the crux of the whole matter, and we need not hesitate to face it frankly and reverently.

There are two ways by which we may know where human thought ends and the divine thought is revealed: by insight and by experience. And the Bible shows itself to be unique and supreme by both tests. For example, take any great book and one can tell instantly, not only by the sweep and rhythm and majesty of certain pages where the thought of the writer passes beyond itself, but also by the response which it evokes in depths of his own soul. For the thoughts of man at their highest and purest carry in them, as the clouds carry the sunlight, the thoughts of the eternal. Further than this we cannot go, unless it be in that amazing sentence in the *Morals on the Book of Job*, by St. Gregory, where, in speaking of the manner in which God makes Himself known to the angels, he writes:

"For because no corporeal obstacle is in the way of a spiritual being, God speaks to His holy angels in the very act of His revealing to their hearts His inscrutable secrets, that whatsoever they ought to do they may read it in the simple contemplation of truth, and that the very delights of contemplation should be like a vocal precept, for that is as it were spoken to them as hearers which is inspired in them as beholders."

Beyond these words no one may venture into the ineffable mystery of the revelation of God to men or angels; and that is why the Bible, albeit a book of the people which were of old, is eternal, fresh as the morning light, exempt from the touch of time because it is timeless. Often it resembles the natural world in its elevation and depressions, but in its great hours it speaks for eternity in words childlike in simplicity, awful in their clarity, and we know, by the mighty answer of our own hearts, that we are listening to the truth about life and death. Whether it be the story of the wayfarer dreaming on a stony bed, the commands of a moral lawgiver in the wilderness, the sob of a Psalmist in his sin, the prophetic vision of Isaiah, or the words of Him who spake as never man spake, when we read it we cry out, as Kepler did when he looked through his glass into the sky, "O Lord, I think Thy thoughts after Thee."

Moreover, by the testimony of ages of human living, the moral teachings of the Bible, and its laws of the life of the spirit, have shown themselves to be among the things that cannot be shaken. Nations disregard them, and fall into ruin. Men defy them, and die in the dust. Even to-day, in these new and changed times, the pages of the Hebrew prophets might be wet with fresh tears because of the sorrows of the broken and fallen in our midst. The experience of humanity in its moral victory and defeat becomes, in this way, a witness to the supremacy of the Bible, confirming alike its spiritual vision and its system of moral values. It is therefore that the Bible lives, not by fiat, but because it is the Book of Eternal

Life in the midst of time, and of its influence and power there will be no end.Between the Old and New Testament there is a gulf, not only as to time, but as to the manner in which God is revealed, as if the river of life, having run under ground for a space, had burst forth into a fountain of light and healing. If in the Old Testament we are shown the contrast between God and man—His greatness and our littleness, His-eternity and our pathetic mortality—the New Testament reveals the kinship of God and man. Communion with God in the New Testament is not, as in the Old, a dialogue of one person with another, but the infusion of a new life by an indwelling spirit. As Luther said long ago, the supreme office of the Bible is to show us Christ, and in Him is all that we need to know even if we never see any other book.

Again, to state the fact is to prove it. Surely the life of Christ, as incomparable in its art as it is ineffable in its revelation of what lies at the heart of this dark world, sets the Bible apart as forever supreme and unapproachable. So much is this so, indeed, that it seem as needless to discuss the uniqueness of the Bible as to defend it from assault. If one will not hear that Biography of Love, that Memoir of Pity, that historic record of Redeeming Grace, neither will he believe though one arise from the dead. There is disclosed the heart of the eternal, the crowning glory of the Bible, and the sovereign beauty of the world; at once a revelation and a redemption. As St. Jerome put it in the preface to his Commentary on Isaiah: "If, according to St; Paul, Christ is 'the power of God and the wisdom of God' one who knows not the Scriptures knows not that power and wisdom; for ignorance of the Scriptures is ignorance of Christ." If the spirit of Jesus is more diffused now than when Jerome Wrote, it is still true that our life and literature, so far as they are imbued with His truth, reflect the light of the Gospels.

Add now the twenty centuries of high, heroic religious experience, so rich, so radiant, so profound, deriving, as it so gratefully confesses, from the story of the life of Christ in the Bible, and the testimony is transcendent! Here the facts are overwhelming, so that he who runs may read, showing that wherever the Bible goes there go light and hope, and noble human living-tenderness in the family, righteousness in the state, and honor among men. What the Bible has meant to our poor humanity, and will yet mean to unknown ages hidden in the womb of time, by virtue of its power to cleanse the sinful, heal the broken of heart, and lift into faith and love those attacked by despair, wasted by weariness, or worn with grief, no mortal pen can recite. Take a single page from the story of the Bible in New Guinea, typical of ten thousand volumes of Christian history, and it tells us facts more to be prized than the discovery of a new star in the sky:

"I have myself seen murderers and cannibals live peaceful lives. I have seen shameless thieves and robbers become honest; I have seen the lascivious and filthy become pure; I have seen the quarrelsome and selfish become kind and gentle. But I have never heard of such changes arising from any other agency than that of the Word whose entrance bringeth life, and whose acceptance is the power of God unto salvation."

Now and again a great heroic soul, or some humble, obscure saint, shows us what life is when the Bible is translated into character-how it makes God real and near, investing these fleeting days with enduring significance and sanctity; how it strengthens what is weak, softens what is hard, and touches the whole nature to beauty and fineness; how it fortifies the soul against those blind fears which no one can name but which make a secret terror in the way; how it heals those profound sorrows of which we hardly dare to speak, not by mere lapse of time nor the induration of the heart, but by transfiguring the old tenderness into a new solace; and how, at last, it flings an arch of promise across the all-devouring grave, linking our mortal life with a life that shall end, less be.

I have not finished, but I must stop. It is of no use to go on. I feel that what hovers before me, although it is so vivid, is not to be told save by the Bible itself, which, as I said at the outset, needs no one to speak for it. Nay, it is the Bible that speaks in my behalf, and as I listen debate ceases, difficulties are forgotten, anxiety disappears, and I am as a child in the arms of One Who knows what I am, whence I came, why I am here, and whither I go, and Who smiles at my terrors.

CHAPTER III
THE WORD OF GOD

FROM end to end, the Bible is a unity in faith, in Spirit, and in purpose, yet It nowhere speaks of itself as a whole. It is too wise, too modest, too intent on the great story it has to tell. Nor does it ever call itself the Word of God... Indeed, it is a striking fact that in the Bible the name "Word of God" is never once applied to anything written. No, the Word of God is living, active, creative, a seed, a fire, a light, a power at once august and intimate, and no book, nor all the books in the world, can contain it. Every land, every people, every age hears it, each in its own tongue, and because there are always listening ears, however few,

One accent of the Holy Ghost
The heedless world has never lost.

The Word of God is eternal. It spoke to man before he had learned to write; it will still speak when all books are faded and forgotten. Heaven and earth may pass away, but the Word of God I will not fail of fulfilment. "All flesh is grass, and all the glory of man as the flower of the grass. The grass withereth and the flower thereof falleth away, but the Word of God endureth forever." What God has to say to man, and what at last He actually did say, is something too great, to wonderful for any human words, even the most eloquent or searching or patient, ever to tell. It is a Living Word, not known by pronunciation, but only by incarnation. As it has been written: "God, who at sundry times and in divers manners spake in times past unto our fathers by the prophets, hath in these last days spoken unto us by His Son. The word was made flesh, and dwelt among us, and we beheld His glory, full of grace and truth."

What, then, is the Bible? It is a record of the God-revealing experiences of the poets, prophets, and apostles of a noble people, as they learned of God through long, tragic ages and wrote what they had learned. Not in writings primarily, but in living history, in actual life, God shows Himself to men. From the Bible we learn not only the truth made known in ancient time, but the method by which it was revealed, and the one is hardly less vital than the other. God spoke to the people which were of old, as He speaks to-day, if we have ears to hear, through life, through facts and events and actions and persons, through history and reflection, and the Bible tells us of the life and action, both personal and national, in which He was revealed. Thus God speaks in the Bible, but He does not write. Then, as now, it was revelation through experience, and the value of the Bible is not only that it tells us what men learned of God in the long ago, but that it helps us to read His newer Word as it is written in the events and actions of to-day.

Here lies the answer to those two profound questions: Does God speak to man to-day? If so, how? Primarily, men are inspired, not writings. Wherever a man, by any means soever, learns what reality is, and what are the laws of the world, he is reading the Word of God. Often he can decipher only here a line and there a stanza, but God is speaking to him. Thus, when Job passed through his bitter trial he learned a new Word of God about suffering, namely, that suffering is not always punishment; and he was able to utter it in a drama that has in it the wide spaces of the desert, its lucid skies, its loneliness and storm. When David was an outcast, a fugitive hunted and pursued, finding shelter in caves, he learned that God lives in the heart more than in places, and he told in song what he had learned in sorrow. When the king died and the nation was shaken, and men felt the insecurity of all things mortal, it was given Isaiah to look through that event and see One who never dies and a throne that cannot be shaken; and he made record of his vision. When Jeremiah was left to stand alone in defiance of the people whom he loved—one of the grandest and most tragic figures in history—he made a new adventure in prayer, and rose above book-religion to life-religion; as, later, the Prophet of the Exile discovered, in the dark night of his sorrow, the Suffering Servant of God walking the dreamy ways of prophecy.

After this manner the Bible was written, slowly and painfully; not so much written as wrought out amid the struggle and sorrow of human life, each page lived before it was written—each line, as Whitman said, wet with human tears. Hence the power that is in it which passes like fire from heart to heart down the ages; and hence, also, the close connection between this Book and the living and abiding word of God. No other book has such power to comfort and command. A famous Master of Balliol has told us that we should "read the Bible as we read any other book"; and that is the surest way to learn that it is unlike any other book. The Bible is literature, if by that we mean "the lasting expression in words of the meaning of life"; but it is something more. It is not art, it is life. Men feel this to be so. Let a man try to read the Bible as literature only, and he will find that in the drama which it unfolds there can be no spectators, no lookers on. Everybody—the reader included—is drawn into the action; each must take sides or make "the great refusal." Something reaches out from its pages and pulls us into the play of its realities. It is not a fiction of what life might have been; it is life itself speaking to us.

Nor is this to disparage literature and its service to the human spirit. Far from it. How we love to wander in its Chamber of Imagery, amid forms lovely and haunting, where Homer sings, and Plato speaks, and Hamlet dies; and there are lines in the great poets—often, even, in lesser poets—which open, in the light of a Hash, a vista half on earth and half in heaven. Literature is beautiful and benign, free, ideal, and richly rewarding. But the Bible is more compelling than persuasive. It does not entertain; it commands. It is too serious, too earnest, too honest to care for art for the sake of art. Its art is artless, its purpose being to lay hold of the heart, the conscience, the will, bringing to the service and solace of man the truth made known in the agony and bloody sweat of mortal life. When a man tries to read the Fifty-first Psalm as he reads any other poem, he finds himself face to face with God and the soul, humbled, subdued, rebuked, exalted. He will not doubt its inspiration; the sense that he is one with that long-dead singer will melt his heart, and he will say, if he be wise, "This thing is of God." Such is the power of the Bible, as unique as it is searching, and if we let it have its way with us, yielding our souls to its passion for righteousness, and its sense of the Eternal Life in Time, it will lead us infallibly in the way everlasting.

Yes, infallibly. Argument is not needed; the fact proves it. The Bible grew up out of a religious life, rich, profound, revealing, and if rightly used and obeyed it will reproduce in us, infallibly, the kind of life which produced it. No other kind of infallibility is needed. Strong men, serious men who wish to fight the battle of character through to something like decency, ask for no surer token. As the Bible is a Book of Life, so its verity and value are to be known only in the midst of life. Experience is the final test. "The word is very nigh unto thee, in thy mouth, and in thy heart, that thou mayest do it." Texts often tell us their meaning if we turn them over, and if we invert this text we learn that the word that is nigh unto us, in our mouths, and in our hearts, is the Word of God. Evermore the challenge of Jesus, is, if we do, we shall know. The writers of the Bible did not argue; they obeyed. They lived before they wrote. They were men of like passions as ourselves, of like faiths and fears and failings. They wrestled with reality; they were sorely tried, and their cries of anguish echo to this day — deathless trumpets from the oblivion of olden time. In weakness they were made strong; in darkness they saw "the brightness on the other side of life"; in death they were not dismayed. They show us in actual life, in outward experience and inward realization, how the victory is won-how truth is learned by living.

Here, in this wise and faithful Book, is the very stuff of life itself; the human realities out of which, not as a theory, but as a fact, faith in God grows. How many they are! The two characters of this Book are the Sky and the Dirt. Its story is the romance of God and man and their eternal life together. Sunrise, sunset, summer, autumn, winter, calm, storm, birth, marriage, love, laughter, pain, sorrow, sin, repentance, the broken heart and the open grave—these old, familiar, human things live in the Bible against a background of Eternity. Those men of old needed guidance as they faced the mystery of life and realized how many questions remain unanswered. They needed comfort in sorrow, courage in disappointment, hope in failure. They needed forgiveness for sin, inspiration in monotony and companionship as one by one their friends dropped away, leaving them to walk alone. Above all they needed light as they looked out upon the world of their day, so tangled and so troubled, and were tempted to despair of finding a way out. They found what they needed in God, and in God alone, and set down in simple words what they learned of His will, His care, His plans for them and their duty to Him. God was made known to them in heroic experience, in sins forgiven, in minds made clear of earthly mists, in hearts healed of the old hurt of life—that dumb and nameless pain that throbs at the heart of our being as we march or creep or crowd through the welter of war, poverty, disease, and death.

What about our own day? This, at least: God is not the great I WAS, but the great I AM, and His Word speaks to us to-day, as of old, through the facts, the events, the actions, the persons of our time, in actual life as it unfolds, in history as it is wrought out in blood and fire and tears. "This day hath this Scripture been fulfilled in your ears," not as some one event was foreshadowed in the imagery of Ezekiel or the visions of the Apocalypse, but as the same laws of righteousness which ruled in the past fulfil themselves anew in the outworking of events-in the overthrow of injustice, in the triumph of right over might, in the deliverance of the poor and the afflicted. "God is not dumb that He should speak no more." He who awakened the soul of Israel and lifted Isaiah to a purer vision through the march of the Assyrian army must have some word to speak to us in the upheavals and overturnings of our day. Manifestly, it is a word not only for our individual leading, but for humanity in its collective life, if we have the insight to read and interpret it. But who is sufficient for these things?

How can we read aright the strange, troubled, tragic history of our own day? Here the Bible is our surest guide, prophet, and friend, if we would trace the ways of God in the "long-lived storm of great events in our own day," since His newer Word must confirm the old, fulfilling itself in the processes of the years. The mighty prophets were the first to see that events do not run wild, but are held and guided by an unseen Hand. Not only one nation, but as their vision broadened, all nations, all lands, all ages, were seen to be subject to Divine-control; all events of history—the march of armies, the fate of dynasties, the fall of cities—are at the bidding of His will. Assyria was a razor to cut away things outgrown. Egypt was a pruning hook. There is no fact today, however appalling, that those watchers of the ways of God did not face. Then, as now, the hills trembled and the uproar of the people was like the roaring of the sea, but they saw God in all, through all, over all. They discerned, now dimly, now clearly, the moral, social, and spiritual purpose of God in history, and it is thus that their Book of Vision is a light to our feet in this far-off age.

God was made known to the prophets and apostles, as He is revealed to-day, in living history as "a creative Personality, a dauntless Saviour, the Builder of a brotherly social order, the universal and eternal good-will." Today we must think out anew our faith in God, not only as that faith is related to our individual struggle for the good, but as it involves a new sense of the relation of nations to one another, and their unity of interest and obligation. In a terrible textbook we have been reading the Word of God that He has "made of one blood every nation of men," and that there is no security, no peace, until we learn to do justly, to love mercy, and to walk humbly before Him. Surely, if God is revealed by the action of events, we shall miss His living word if the terrible events of the last ten years do not evoke in us a larger thought and a kindlier feeling toward all races of men, thereby interpreting the solidarity of humanity in which all peoples are members one of another. It must be the clear will of God by these, His acts, to lead us toward the fulfilment of that vision, so often foretold in the Bible, when

> Nation with nation, land with land,
>   Unarmed shall live as comrades free;
> In every heart and brain shall throb
>   The pulse of one fraternity.

Again, it must be that a revealing Word of God is speaking to our humanity, if it will but listen, in its suffering, its misery, and in the voice of its weeping for the dead. Here, too, the tender heart of the Bible is true to our deep need, and its leaves are for our healing. After all, our woe is new only in its magnitude, not in its quality. Hunger is hunger, pain pain, death death the world over; in Judea as in England. The seers of old saw in suffering not a sign of the forgetfulness of God, still less a proof of His weakness or of His indifference, but the Cloud of His Presence. Nay, more: the supreme surprise of the Bible, that which. filled its writers with a wonder beyond words, is that God suffers with man and for man. Here we enter where words cannot follow. Even the stately, awe-struck words of the Prophet of the Exile, forever memorable in their beauty; do not tell half the depth and richness of this truth. Only a Living Word made flesh, pure, heroic, lovely, tried and found true, suffering but victorious, walking by our side, laying His hand upon our sickness, cooling our fever, cleansing, teaching, enfolding, upholding, can tell the whole truth.

Yes, the poet was right; God may have other words for other worlds, but His supreme Word for this world, yesterday, to-day, forever, is Christ! He is the central Figure of the Bible, its crown, its glory, its glow-point of vision and revelation. Take Him away and its light grows dim. He fulfilled the whole Book, its history, its poetry, its prophecy, its ritual, even as He fulfils our deepest yearning and our highest hope. Ages have come and gone, but He abides—abides because He is real, because He is unexhausted, because He is needed. Little is left today save Christ—Himself smitten and afflicted, bruised of God and wounded—but He is all we need. If we hear Him, follow Him, obey Him, we shall walk together into a new world wherein dwelleth righteousness and love-He is the Word of God.

CHAPTER IV
OUR ENGLISH BIBLE

WHAT Homer was to the Greeks, and the Koran to the Arabs, that, and much more, the English Bible is to us. It is the mother of our literary family, and if some of its children have grown up and become very wise in their own conceit, none the less they rejoice to gather about its knee and pay tribute.

But to regard the Bible simply as a literary classic, apart from what it has been to the faiths and hopes and prayers of men, and its inweaving into the intellectual and spiritual life of a great race, is to confuse effect with cause. There is a danger lest these deeper meanings, these solemn and precious associations, be transferred to the Bible as pure literature and we be found praising too highly as English style what was first a religious and historical experience. Not only was the Bible the loom on which our language was woven, but it is a pervasive, refining, redeeming force bequeathed to us, with whatsoever else that was good and true, in the very fibre of our being. As Father-Faber has said, in a passage of singular eloquence and insight:

"It lives on the ear like a music that can never be forgotten, like the sound of church bells which one scarcely knows how he can forego. The memory of the dead passes into it. The potent traditions of childhood are stereotyped in its verses. It is the representative of a man's best moments; all that there is about him of soft and gentle and pure and penitent and good speaks to him forever out of his English Bible. There is not a Protestant with one spark of religiousness about him whose spiritual biography is not in his Saxon Bible."

In 1604 King James, soon after his accession, convened the Hampton Court conference, to consider "things pretended to be amiss in the church." On the second day Reynolds, the

Puritan leader, suggested a new translation of the Bible to take the place of those then extant. There was some debate, but it set on fire the fancy of the king, who had an itch for repute as a scholar, and who, under the tutorship of Buchanan, had already been working at the Psalms in verse. The outcome was the appointment of a body of revisors, some forty-seven in number, which was divided into six companies of which two were to sit at Cambridge, two at Oxford, and two at Westminster. They were to make a uniform version, answering to the original, to be read in the churches and no other. No marginal notes, except for philological purposes, were permitted, as the book was not to be controversial, but the work of all who loved and honored the Bible, unbiased by sectarian feuds.

Not many of the revisors are otherwise known to fame, though some of them attained to high office in the church. Among them were Andrews, Overal, Reynolds, Abbott, Barlow, and Miles Smith, who wrote "the learned and religious preface to the translation." Few details as to the exact order of procedure have come down to us, and never, perhaps, has a great enterprise of like nature been carried out with so little information preserved of the laborers, their method, and manner of work. We know, however, that the work of revision occupied two years and nine months, and that use was made of all extant versions, including the Rheimish Version, from which, for example, was derived that felicitous phrase, "the ministry of reconciliation." The purpose of the revisors was thus stated, and it was reverent, far-reaching, and wise: "We never thought, from the beginning, that we should need to make a new translation, nor yet to make a bad one good, but out of many good ones one principal good one, not justly to be excepted against—that hath been our endeavor, that our mark."

And it is to this principle that our version owes its unrivalled merits. Like a costly mosaic, besides having its own felicities, it inherited the beauties of all the versions that went before.

Some time in 1611, "after long expectation and great desire," says Fuller, the new Version appeared, printed by Robert Barker, marred only by the inaccuracies inevitable at that period, and a too adulatory dedication to the king. While there is no record that it was ever publicly sanctioned by convocation, privy councilor king - due" perhaps, to the great fire in 1618-it soon superseded all other versions, by virtue of' its own inherent superiority, and by the middle of the next century it had become "the undisputed Bible of the English people." Nor can it ever be moved from its honored and secure position in our religious and literary history. There need not have been a Revised Version; all that was needed, apart from the quiet process of revision, steadily going on, was to correct obvious errors in the light of later textual research. The Version of 1881, while it erased many blemishes, falls far below the stately English of the King James Bible, which is still the familiar friend of the fire side and the closet.

As a feat of translation, the Version of 1611 is unique and unmatched in the annals of literature. It is faithful not only to the letter, but to the spirit of the original, and yet it is truly an English book. Its words are in bulk Saxon, the Lord's Prayer in Matthew, for instance, having fifty-nine of its words pure English, thirty-five Saxon undefiled, and only six of Latin origin. More wonderful still is the fact that, while it used English words, it kept not only the phrases, but the flavor, spirit and essence of the language wherein the Bible was born—a feat which, as Coleridge says, "almost makes us think that the translators themselves were inspired." Indeed, it may be said that the Bible was rather transferred to the English language than translated into it. That cannot be said of Homer, or of any other book that has found its way into our speech, and the reason for it was that for a thousand years the Bible had lived in the hearts of the English people, had helped to mould their language, to shape their character, and to make them what they were. As Taine pointed out, the temper of the people receiving the Book was so in harmony with that of the people from whom it came, that it seemed more like a native growth than an exotic. This could not be again in just the same way; but that it was so once is a fact beyond all thought or thankfulness. By a rare blend of circumstances we are permitted to hear the music of the Bible almost as if the original artists were playing it. One feels this in reading the Gospels, and still more in the Old Testament, but most of all perhaps, when he hears, like echoes from afar,

> "The chime of rolling rivers,
> Through the forest of the Psalms."

Back of 1611 lay a long, heroic, aspiring history—from the time when Caedmon, the forlorn cowherd, fell asleep under the stars, and was bidden to sing the Bible story, down to the year when Shakespeare left London for his home on the Avon. It had been the wish of King Alfred that the young men of his realm might read the Bible in their own language, and he left an unfinished version of the Psalms when he died. But his wish had to wait until a crude and stammering tongue grew into a rich and musical speech - until the tapestry was woven on which the Bible writers could work their designs. Such weavers as Aldhelm, Bede, Elfric, Wyclif, and Purvey drew their threads equally from the Bible itself and from the life of the people, until the imagery of the Book was wrought into the very fibre of the language. No other book was ever so interwoven with the life of a people, at once their supreme literary classic and the message of their Maker to their souls.

THE GREAT LIGHT

At last came Tyndale-the one great figure in the story of our English Bible — whose aim it was to make "the ploughboy know more about the Scripture than the priest does to-day." Set on fire by the spirit of God and the genius of Erasmus, by the aid of the printing press he made and published the version which was the basis of the Bible as we know and love it. Hunted as a heretic, beset by spies, he toiled in behalf of the Bible for the people, in the language of the people in the belief that the humblest soul, when left alone with the Bible, can find the way, the truth, and the life. With an industry unwearying, and a faith unwavering, he worked amid peril and often in the shadow of death, and at last gave his life for the Bible that we might give our

lives to it. Of his version Froude wrote in a famous passage:

"Though since that time it has been many times revised and altered, we may say that it is substantially the Bible with which we are familiar. The peculiar genius which breathes through it, the mingled tenderness and majesty, the Saxon simplicity, the preternatural grandeur — unequaled, unapproached, in the attempted improvements of modem scholars — all are here, and bear the impress of the mind of one man, William Tyndale. Lying, while engaged in that great office, under the shadow of death, the sword above his head and ready at any moment to fall, he worked, under circumstances alone perhaps truly worthy of the task which was laid upon him — his spirit, as it were, divorced from the world, moved in a purer element than common air."

There was a time when the Bible formed almost the only literature of England; and today, if it were taken away, that literature would be torn to shreds and tatters. If we except a few tracts of Wyclif, all the prose literature of England has grown up since the Tyndale version was made. There was practically no history in the English tongue, no romance, and hardly any poetry, save the little-known verse of Chaucer, when the Bible was set up in the churches. Truly did Macaulay say, in his essay on Dryden, that if everything else in our language should perish, the Bible would alone suffice to show the whole extent of its beauty and power. Edmund Spenser put himself to school in the prophetic music of the Bible in order to write *Faerie Queen*, and Milton learned his song from the same choir. Carlyle, though he truncated his faith, had in his very blood, almost without knowing it, the rhapsody and thought of the prophets—their sense of the infinite, of the awfulness of God, of the blindness and littleness of man, of the sarcasm of providence, of those invisible influences which give depth and meaning to human sorrow and joy—which he had heard so often from the fireside Bible; as Burns, before him, had learned from the same book his truth of the indestructibleness of honor, of the humanness of the Divine Father drawing the divine in humanity toward it, which made his verse throb with the power and passion of tears. Whole volumes have been filled with the allusions to the Bible in Shakespeare, Scott, Ruskin, and Dickens, and others might be made from the writings of Eliot, Thackeray, Stevenson, Swinburne, and even Thomas Hardy. The Bible sings in our poetry, chants in our music, echoes in our eloquence, from Webster to Lincoln, and in our tragedy flashes forever its truth of the terribleness of sin, the failure of godless self-keeping, and the forlorn wandering of the soul that drifts, blinded away from virtue. As Watts-Dunton said in his great essay on the Psalms:

"The Bible is going to be eternal. For that which decides the vitality of any book is precisely that which decides the value of any human soul - not the knowledge it contains, but simply the attitude it assumes towards the universe, unseen as well as seen. The attitude of the Bible is just that which every soul must, in its highest and truest moods, always assume—that of a wise wonder in front of such a universe as this—that of noble humility before a God such as He in

THE GREAT LIGHT

Whose great hand we stand. This is why—like the mirror of Alexander, like that most precious cup of Jemshid, imagined of the Persians - the Bible reflects today, and will reflect forever, every wave of human emotion, every passing event of human life-reflect them as faithfully as it did to the great and simple people in whose great and I simple tongue it was written."

Here is a book whose scene is the sky and the dirt, and all that lies between—a book of the open air in which seas ebb and flow, and mountains lift their peaks, and rivers shine in the sunlight, and flowers bloom, and birds sing, and suns rise and set, and forests cover the hills like the shadow of God. It is the most human of books, telling the secrets of the soul, its bitter pessimism and its death-defying hope, its pain, its passion, its sin, its sobs, and its song, as it moves "amid encircling gloom" from the cradle to the grave—tells all, without malice and without mincing words, in the grand style that can do no wrong, while echoing the sweet-toned pathos of the pity of God. Not a page of it, as Walt Whitman said in a superb passage, not a verse of it, not a word of it, but has been drenched with the life-blood of some patient, heroic, aspiring, God-illumined soul. No other book is so honest with us, so mercilessly merciful, so austere, and yet so tender, piercing to the dividing of marrow and bone, yet healing the deep wounds of sin and sorrow.

Above all, it tells of Him who lived "the human life of God" on earth—how the Eternal Word became flesh and dwelt among us in grace and truth, whose life is the light of men and whose words scatter the dark confusions of the grave, while showing us the immutable duty of love to God and man. It is a book to take to the heart; to turn to in hours of joy; to look into in times of sorrow; and to accept at all times as our friend, teacher, and guide- a book of faith: hope and love, whose song of the soul, beginning in faint, wistful notes, gathers volume and melody until it swells into the great choruses of the Apocalypse, which Tennyson used to recite with trembling voice and transfigured face, and which Jowett said are better in English than in Greek. If we are ignorant, it will tell us all we need to know of God, duty, and the life beyond the tomb; if we are lost, it will bring us home; if the inner light burns low, it will kindle these poor hearts of ours with a flame from the altar of God.

What a gift to our English race, what a treasure incalculable and imperishable"a well of English undefiled," limpid, clear, and deep; a monument to our martyrs; the masterpiece of our literature; the storehouse of historic memories and prophecies; the revelation of the will of God concerning us—how we should love it, read it, and be happy with it! When Sir Walter Scott was dying he asked Lockhart to read to him aloud. "From what book?" came the not unnatural question-and what a lesson for our children in the simple answer: "There is but one Book."

"Behold I stand at the door and knock; if any man hear my voice and open the door, will come in to him, and will sup with him, and he with me. And the spirit and the bride say, come. And he that heareth, let him say, come. And he that is athirst, let him come; and whosoever will, let him come and take of the water of life freely."

CHAPTER V
THE GREAT LIGHT

No Mason need be told the place of honor which the Bible has in Masonry. It is the Great Light of the Lodge, the center, source and symbol of the truth Masonry is trying to teach. Upon the Altar, supporting the Square and Compasses, it shines, at once a kindly Light to lead and a holy Law to command. The Bible opens when the Lodge opens; it closes when the Lodge closes. No Lodge can transact its own business, much less initiate candidates into its mysteries, unless the Bible lies open upon its Altar. Thus the book of Holy Law rules the Lodge in its labors, as the Sun rules the day, making its work a worship.

Therein our gentle Craft is wise, building its philosophy upon faith in spiritual verity and ruling its conduct by the immutable principles of moral obligation. While Masonry is not a religion, in the sense that it is one religion among many, it is none the less religious in its spirit and purpose: not simply a code of ethics, but a system of moral mysticism—its teaching transfigured by the truth which lies behind all the sects and religions and yet. peculiar to none.[1] It seeks to

---

[1]

Whether Masonry is in any sense a religion is a moot question into which we need not go here. Some hold that it is in no sense a religion, but simply a system of ethics taught by symbols, emblems and allegories. Others contend that it is not only religious but, historically and spiritually, a distinctly Christian institution. (*The Religion of Freemasonry*, by H. J. Whymper.) It all depends, of course, on what we mean by a religion. My own attitude is very much in accord with that of Brother J. S. M. Ward in his *Freemasonry, its Aims and Ideals*; that Masonry is not a religion, much less a church or a sect, but that it is essentially religious: not a religion, but Religion.

develop moral and spiritual life, to purify thought, to refine and exalt character-in short to build men and then make them Brothers and Builders; and to that end it takes the Bible as its Guide, Prophet,. and Friend.

Let us rather say that Masonry, as we see it in our dream and seek to realize it in our fellow. ship, is like one of the cathedrals which our Brethren built in the olden time: faith its foundation, righteousness its corner stone, strength and wisdom its walls, beauty its form and fashion, brotherly love its clasped arches, reverence its roof, the Bible its Altar Light, mysticism its music, charity its incense, fellowship its sacrament, its symbols windows nobly wrought, half. revealing and half-concealing a Truth too elusive for words, too vast for dogma, and too bright for eyes unveiled, and only hinted to us until we are ready and worthy to behold it with other and clearer eyes than now we know.

I

The, history of the Bible in the life and symbolism of Masonry is a very interesting story, and we may trace it in some detail, if only to reveal the development of the Craft and how the Holy Book came to its place of power and command. Originally, to go no further back than the Middle Ages, Masonry was not only a Christian but a Catholic institution. Whatever it may have been before our era is not now our concern, but in the Middle Ages our Brethren were Christian craftsmen toiling in the service of the Church—the only church then in existence, save a few heroic and persecuted sects deemed heretical and reckoned outside the pale of the Christian community. The Mason guilds, like other guilds of the period, were intensely religious, each haying its patron saint, and each its festivals when candles were burned and prayers offered at a shrine. [1]

---

[1] English Guilds, by Toulmin Smith.

The Great Light

Indeed, the oldest document of the Craft, the Halliwell Manuscript—better known as the Regius Poem—dated about 1390, is not only Christian but definitely Catholic. Halliwell, its discoverer, held that it was written by a priest, and it is such a document as a priest might have written, opening with an invocation to the Trinity and the Virgin Mary, devoted to the religious instruction of the Craft, including the proper way to celebrate the Mass. There were, to be sure as at all other times—a number of cults, sects and schools of various kinds, within the Church and outside, devoted to occultism, mysticism, and different systems of symbolism, and no doubt these influenced the Craft to some degree; but as a whole Freemasons were loyal churchmen, and remained so throughout the cathedral-building period.

Let it be remembered that in the church of that time, as in the same church to-day, the Bible was not the supreme authority in matters of religious faith and practice. The Church, not the Book, was the court of final appeal, and this fact. was reflected in the documents of the Craft. While the Bible is mentioned in some of the old Manuscripts of the Fraternity, and had a place of honor as the book upon which the oath of a Mason was taken, it is nowhere referred to as a Great Light of the Lodge. In the Harleian Manuscripts, dated about 1600, the obligation of an initiate closes with the words: "So help me God, and the holy contents of this book." In the old Ritual, of which a copy from the Royal Library in Berlin is given by Krause, there is no mention of the Bible as one of the Lights of the Lodge.

With the advent of the Reformation, toward which many movements in the Church as well as outside had been tending, the whole situation was changed. For whole peoples and a large section of the Church the scepter of religious authority passed from the Church to the Bible, and this fact was also reflected in the history of Masonry. Indeed, we have not duly considered how truly Masonry, in its modern form, was a child of the Reformation, allied, as it was, with the movement, or group of movements, out of which came the freedom of the peoples, the liberty of conscience, and the independence of manhood. From the time of Edward VI on the Craft was emphatically Protestant in its affinities, as is shown by the invocations used in the Old Charges of the period, of which the Harleian Manuscript is a notable instance:

Thou Almighty Father of Heaven, with the Wisdom of the Glorious Sonne, through the goodness of the Holy Ghost, three persons in one Godhead, bee with our beginning and give us grace soe to governe our lives that we may come to his bliss that never shall have end.

But, while Masonry became Protestant in spirit and principle, it still remained Christian—let us not forget that fact—and continued to be distinctly so until a much later time. Naturally, in the Lodge as in the Protestant church, the Bible became supreme, its slow elevation not unlike the elevation of the Square in our Ritual, though, as a fact, not until we reach the Rituals of 1760 do we find it described as one of the three Great Lights of the Lodge. But it was present and its influence and power were manifest, giving basis to the faith of the Craft and color to its rituals and rites, all through the extraordinary period of the "revival" or transformation, of which we know so little and would like to know so much, especially on its religious side.

Just what happened at the time of the so-called "revival" of Masonry in 1717, and in the period immediately following the founding of the Grand Lodge of England, is hard to know. The background is hazy and the records are too scanty and scrappy to enable us to trace the many influences which must have been at work, converging in the Constitutions of 1723, which, as Gould said, "may safely be ascribed to Anderson." It was more than a revival; it was a revolution. It not only gave Masonry a new form and organization, finding focus in the Grand Lodge, but also a new attitude toward the church—an attitude so far-reaching that its full import was not understood until years afterward, and then it made a schism which lasted for more than half a century. Some of us would give much to know what lay behind and led up to the memorable article "Concerning God and Religion" in the Constitutions of 1723. If read in the setting of its age, it was not only revolutionary but prophetic:

A Mason is obliged by his Tenure to obey the moral Law; and if he rightly understands the Art, he will never be a stupid Atheist, nor an irreligious Libertine. But though in ancient Times, Masons were charged in every Country to be of the religion of that Country or Nation, whatever it was, yet 'tis now thought more expedient only to oblige them to that Religion in which all Men agree, leaving their particular opinions to themselves; that is, to be good Men and true, or men of Honor and Honesty, by whatever Denomination or persuasion they may be distinguished; whereby Masonry becomes the Center of Union, and the means of conciliating true Friendship among Persons that must have remained at a perpetual distance.

That is to say, just as in the Reformation Masonry severed its connection with Catholicism, so in 1717 it severed itself once and for all from anyone church, sect, or party creed, making itself henceforth independent of any school of theology. It proposed to unite men upon the common eternal religion in which all men agree, asking Masons to keep "their particular opinions to themselves" and not make them tests of fellowship in Freemasonry. As Burke said, not many men see what is passing before their eyes, and it was true in this instance. Only a few, if any, realized at first how far-reaching such a statement was, but by the middle of the century its meaning was discovered, and the result was the organization of a rival Grand Lodge in 1751, calling itself "Ancient," on the ground that the "Modern" Grand Lodge had abandoned the faith. Gould puts it very aptly when he says that "this drawing of a sponge over the ancient Charge 'to be true to

God and Holy Church was doubtless looked upon by many Masons of those days in very much the same way as we now regard the absence of any religious formulary in the so-called Masonry of the Grand Orient of France": and he might have added, with as little reason. Two rival Grand Lodges existed side by side for fifty years, not always without friction, but the "Moderns" finally won, disengaging Masonry from specific allegiance to anyone religion to the exclusion of all others. In the Lodge of Reconciliation in 1813 the universal religious character of the Craft was affirmed, and the last definite element of Christianity—in its dogmatic theological sense vanished, albeit distinctively Christian prayers were often offered in Lodges, as they are to-day. Not all Masons were satisfied with the solution, and Hutchinson in *The Spirit of Masonry*—a little classic to this day-made plea for a definitely Christian Masonry, as did Oliver and others. Even as late as 1885 the late Brother H. J. Whymper repeated the plea in his able book, *The Religion of Freemasonry*, but to no avail. Never again will Masonry become a mere servant of one religious dogma or creed, but will continue to be "the center of union, and the means of conciliating true friendship" not only among persons but among faiths "that must have remained at a perpetual distance."

Naturally, all this has to do with the place and influence of the Bible in the Craft. During all the divisions and debates the Bible held its place of honor on the Altar of the Lodge, shining the brighter in its inherent majesty as theological and sectarian obscurations were removed. Today it lies upon the Altar, open for all to read, open for each to interpret for himself—a source of strength and a focus of fellowship instead of division and debate. Slowly its power has gathered and grown until it has become itself a symbol of the Will of God for the life of man, the grand ideality of religious faith shining through its cathedral windows, casting a ray of white light upon the issues of character and the awful tide of human circumstance.

II

Freemasonry, to put it simply and plainly, rests upon the Faith which finds 'its deepest, clearest, sanest utterance in the Bible — faith in God the Master Builder of the Universe and the Father of Humanity, by whose grace we live and in whose wise will is our peace and hope. It is a faith which can neither be demonstrated nor argued down, and it is idle to debate about it. No view of life which is of value is ever secured, much less maintained, by debate. Every wise man knows that there is no proof in reason for anything which we fundamentally believe, because reason is not fundamental. Life, not logic, is the basis of faith. Men do not believe in God because they have proved Him; they are always trying to prove Him because they cannot help believing in Him. The Bible does not argue; it opens the window and lets in the Light.

For though God, which is the name we give to the mystery and meaning of life, maybe revealed, He cannot be uttered, and in trying to utter Him we may lose the Unutterable God, maker of heaven and earth and all that in them is, before whom silence is eloquence and wonder is worship. Wisdom lies in trusting the natural, uncorrupted sense of humanity which cannot look abroad upon this world, up into the night sky with its star-light and silence, or listen to the awful voice of moral law within, without realizing that there was Something here before we were here, Something which will be here when we are gone. Happily we are not confronted by a world which mocks our aspiration, but by a universe which invites our thought, and is interpretable, as every science makes plain, as far as we are able to go by our minds; and it is only sound sense to conclude that such a world is an embodiment and expression of Mind.

What is more wonderful and awful is that the Mind within and behind the moving panorama of the world is a

Mind akin to our own, else we would stare at the world in blank and perpetual amazement, unable to read a line of its legend. If, now, one door yields to our inquiry, and another door opens at our knock, and another and another; if amid the tragedy of life we discover in the universe and in ourselves that which enables us to endure and triumph over the worst that life can do to us, defying disaster in the name of right; if beside an open grave we find that in our hearts which refuses to let death have the last word; surely it requires only a certain robustness of spirit—that is, Faith—to believe, that, if not yet by us, why, then, mayhap by those who come after us, or by ourselves in some state of being in which we shall be no longer restrained by the weakness of mortality, or befogged by the mists and illusions of time, the mind of man shall find itself at home and unafraid in the great universe of God—a citizen of a City that hath foundations. Hear now the authentic voice of the ancient faith of humanity and the echo of its answer in the Book of Revelation:

Oh, that I knew where I might find Him! I would order my cause before Him, and fill my mouth with arguments.

Be still and know that I am God. If thou seek the Lord thy God with all thy heart thou shalt find him.

Wherewithal shall a young man cleanse his way? Who shall dwell in Thy holy hill?

What doth the Lord require of thee, but to do justly, to love mercy, and to walk humbly with thy God?

Lord, what wilt Thou have me to do? Show me Thy way; teach me Thy law.

Whatsoever ye would that men should do to you, do ye even so to them: this is the

law and the prophets.

If a man die, shall he live again? Is there hope in the grave?

In my Father's house are many mansions. If it were not so, I would have told you.

III

What, now, does this mighty faith mean for us here and now? Obviously it means that we are here in the world to do something, to build something, to become something; and what we build or become ought to express and perpetuate our personality. There is a kind of immortality which we should all earn in the world, by so building our lives into the order of things that whatever immortality this world shall have our character shall have a share in it. In the end of the days the Father-Judge of all the earth shall ask us what we did, with such faculties and opportunities as life gave us. Once, in the south of England, I heard a little song which seemed to me to have in it a bit of final philosophy:

> The good Lord made the earth and the sky,
> The rivers and the sea, and me.
> He made no roads; but here am I as happy as can be.
> It's just as though He'd said to me,
>   "John, there's the job for thee."

There is a deep Truth in that rhyme, for in a sense God has completed nothing; not because he has not the power or the will, but out of a kind of respect for man, so to put it, offering us a share in his work of creation. He makes no roads. He builds no houses. He provides the materials; he furnishes the foundations; but the road and the house must be the work of man. Edwin Markham, a good gray poet of our Craft, was right when he wrote:

> We men of earth have here the stuff
> Of Paradise-we have enough!
> We need no other stones to build
> The stairs into the Unfulfilled-
> No other ivory for the doors-

No other marble for the floor&-
No other cedar for the beam
And dome of man's immortal dream.
Here on the paths of every day-
Here on the common human way-
Is all the busy gods would take
To build a heaven, to mould and make
New Edens. Ours the task sublime
To build Eternity in Time!

By the same token, if we are to build to any purpose, or with any hope of permanence, we must build upon the Will of God. The truth that there is a Will within everything and over everything has too little place in our thought; hence our impatience, our restlessness, and our liability to panic. The first fact of experience, if not the final truth of philosophy, is that the world has a mind of its own, which the Bible calls the Will of God. Manifestly we must live and build in harmony with the laws and forces of the world, if we expect our house to endure. Otherwise it rests upon sand, and the Hoods will sweep it away. We would not trust ourselves to a house which had been built casually and haphazard, and this must be equally true of the House of the Spirit not built with hands, which we are set to build in the midst of the years. Here also we build wisely only when we build in harmony with the Will of God as we see it and know it, else our proudest fabric totters to ruin.

Manifestly, too, we cannot know the Will of God, much less do it, without the help of God, which we learn in every degree of Masonry to invoke by deliberate acts of worship and prayer, but also by the effort to keep ourselves within the midst of it by regular obedience and fidelity. No Mason of any degree, if he knows his Art, sets out upon any important undertaking without invoking the aid of One who is wiser than himself. We may be sure that God no more wishes us to live without his aid than he wishes us to live without air. He is the air of our spirit. Therefore we are to rebuke ourselves and call ourselves back from any momentary lapse, or from any prolonged neglect, lest we may have gone too far and lost our way. For God hath made us and not we ourselves, and it does not lie in man to direct his steps.

The great things in this world are accomplished neither by our anxieties nor by our ingenuities. By these lower, lesser faculties we may achieve temporary and passing things; but the great, enduring things are accomplished, not, indeed, apart from us, and yet not wholly as the result of our efforts, but by the harmony of our intention and effort with the will and purpose of God. Here is a truth to which we may apply a test any day, anywhere. If we are defeated or harassed or afraid or at a loss, we may direct our minds to God and come upon a world of reality on which we can refound our faith, and confront the difficulties and embarrassments of our days; by which also we may face the vaster problems and mysteries and terrors, it may be, which lie upon all the horizons of life.

IV

What is the will of God for the life of man in the world? To answer that question we must interpret the law of Nature in the light of Revelation; and when we do so we learn that the will of God is the unity of mankind, and His purpose is Brotherhood. When we study the dark, tragic, terrible story of the past, we discover, if we ponder long enough to understand, two laws in seeming conflict—the Law of Mutual Aid and the Law of the Struggle for Existence: but the higher, gentler law slowly triumphs over the lower, lesser law-includes it, indeed, and fulfils it. All the great human gifts and institutions—speech, writing, painting, music, the home, the state, the altar-had one result: they enabled men to unite, to co-operate, to share a common fund of knowledge, a common faith in truth and beauty and goodness. They tended to make multitudes of men into Man, the Race, the Human Family. Clans and classes united into kingdoms, and the spirit of brotherhood grew, precariously amid feuds and wars, carrying forward what Conrad called "the desperate struggle for fraternity against the solitariness and selfishness of mankind." Through all primitive savageries the principle of fraternity was kept alive, and it lay at the root of the human advance; as witness the doom of all attempts to solve the making of a man or a nation in defiance of it.

When we turn to the Great Light upon the Altar we learn what lay back of that slow ascending effort: not blind Fate, not mere Power, not Accident, but Divine Necessity. It was God the Father of men working to realize the Brotherhood of Man, which is the purpose of His will and the dream of His heart. For, if God is our Father then fraternity is not a fiction, but a need of the Divine nature no less than a necessity of human nature. Otherwise we follow a forlorn hope doomed to defeat, and all the higher ideals of man are at the mercy of his lower instincts. It' is as if all the voices of the world had united into one voice of high command: "*Be Brothers, be Builders; live and let live; think and let think; do justly, love mercy; and know that the men of the four seas are kinsmen.*" Here lies the foundation of fraternity, the inspiration and assurance of the final enterprise of humanity-to build a Brotherly World.

Here, too, lies the basis of Masonry, its place and part and meaning in the world, its mission being to teach men to obey the will of God, to build upon His will by His help, but also that they must build together, as our Brethren built their cathedrals, if the kingdom of heaven is to be established upon earth. Never has this truth been more clearly stated than in a book[1] which a great Craftsman of Scotland left us as a legacy when he climbed ahead to work up in the dome of the Temple; a book wise rather than clever, beautiful rather than brilliant, but with hardly a page that does not yield an insight to illumine, some epigram to haunt the mind; one of the classics of the Craft, simple, lucid, aglow with poetic light and practical wisdom. The beauty of the book is inwrought, not decorative, in the build of its thought even more than in the turn of its sentences, and still more in the radiant moral mysticism which transfigures its teaching. There are passages of ,singular nobility both of language and of thought, as witness this interpretation of the Great Landmark:

Why is Masonry here in this world of selfishness and strife? Wherefore has it been, amid war and incessant conflict, developed along the lines of peace and love; and so marvelously molded and developed that in every land it is known, and by every race made welcome? Has all this been done that it may live for itself alone? No, there on its Trestleboard is the Plan of the Great Architect and its mission is to work out that plan.

Out of the rough hard quarries of quarreling humanity it has to build It Temple of Brotherhood and Peace. This Temple is the great Landmark-the highest and grandest ideal of Masonry. To build, to strengthen and beautify it, we must bring in the aid of all the arts and sciences, apply every resource that civilization and progress can give us, and exercise all the powers and gifts with which we have been endowed.

---

[1]Speculative Masonry, by A. S. McBride.

What nobler work can we be engaged in, Brethren? Yet, how far we are, as a rule, from understanding it? We seem to be groping in the dark. Yet, it is ignorance more than unwillingness that hinders the work. Like the ingenious craftsman at the building of the Temple at Jerusalem, we appear to be without plan and instruction, while, in reality, our plan and instruction lie in the work itself. Then, like him, we shall some day have our reward, and will gratefully exclaim. "Thank God, I have marked well."

V

Plan and instruction we have so long as the Great Light shines in the Lodge, revealing the reality upon which faith is founded, the while it shows us our duty to ourselves and to our fellows, and the direction and destiny of our days. Evermore the Holy Book is central, sovereign, supreme, the master light of all our seeing, a law to our hearts and a path for our feet. From the Altar it pours forth upon the East, the West, the South its white light of spiritual vision, moral law, and immortal hope. Almost every name in our ceremonies is a Bible name, and students have traced about seventy-five references to the Bible in the ritual of the Craft. But more important than direct references is the fact that the spirit of the Bible, its faith, its attitude toward life, pervades Masonry like a rhythm or a fragrance.

As soon as an initiate enters the Lodge he hears the words of the Bible recited as an accompaniment to his advance toward the light. In the First Degree he hears the 133rd Psalm, in which a happy singer of a time far gone celebrates the peace and quiet contented joy of a love-anointed brotherly fellowship, as gentle as the dew descending upon the mountains of God. In the Second Degree he sees in the flashing imagery of the prophecy of Amos a plumb-line held in the hand of God, and let down from heaven to test the work and worth of men and nations. In the Third Degree he listens to a litany of old age and decay, unmatched in any language, describing the slow crumbling of mortal powers and the masterful negation and collapse of the body, until the golden bowl is broken and the pitcher broken at the fountain, and dust returns unto dust, and the spirit takes its long last flight to God who gave it.

And finally, when the shadow of terrifying tragedy falls upon the scene of the drama, when stupid cunning seems to triumph over moral nobility, and heroic integrity is stricken down and buried in the rubbish, leaving man dismayed and appalled, as if his high values were worthless in face of low brute force and foul fact, there is a prayer, one of the greatest in literature—a mosaic of Bible words—gritty hard and bitter in its realism to life, yet touched by the poignant pathos of our mortal lot, pent up in the kingdoms of pity and death, and only redeemed from despair by the hope of man in God who will not let him be utterly cut off, lest something in God die too and chaos come again, and dull death and its devouring grave be victor over all.

However men differ in creed or theology, all good men are agreed that within the covers of the Holy Bible are found those principles of morality which lay the foundation upon which to build a righteous life. Freemasonry therefore opens this book upon its altars, with the command to each of its votaries that he diligently study therein to learn the way to everlasting life. Adopting no particular creed, forbidding sectarian discussion within its Lodge rooms, encouraging each to be stead. fast in the faith of his acceptance. Freemasonry takes all good men by the hand, and, leading them to its altars, points to the open Bible thereon, and urges upon each that he faithfully direct his steps through life by the light he there shall find, , and as he there shall find it.

If from our altars the atheist, the infidel, the irreligious man, or the libertine should ever be able to wrest this Book of Sacred Laws, and thus remove, or even obscure, the greatest

Light in Masonry-that light which for centuries has been the rule and guide of Freemasons-then could we no longer claim for ourselves the rank and title of Free and Accepted Masons; but so long as that Sacred Light shines upon our altars, so long as it illuminates the pathway of the Craftsman by the golden rays of truth, so long and 'no longer can Freemasonry live and shed its beneficent influence upon mankind.

So we read in the Monitor; and they are noble words nobly uttered, setting forth the large outlook and wise tolerance of Freemasonry—a thing for which to thank God in a world of faction and fanaticism—yet affirming the unswerving loyalty of the Craft to the Great Light of the Lodge. But what if the Book of Holy Law lie upon the Altar open but unread, honored but unobeyed, taken as a token but ignored as a teacher? What we have most to fear is not an invasion of the atheist or the infidel, still less the irreligious man and the libertine—neither of whom is interested in our Order, or in any other sacred office—but the ignorance which bows to the no. blest of all books as to a fetish and is blind to its meaning as a faith; the indifference which acknowledges the heavenly vision but remains un. moved; and the idle apathy which mistakes a pious profession of high ideals for an actual performance of high tasks.

CHAPTER VI
READING THE BIBLE
I

IF we make bold and ask the question: How should a Mason read the Bible? the answer is plain enough: He should read it as any other man reads any other book. Already we have quoted the words of Jowett, of Oxford, when he said that to read the Bible as we read any other book is the best way to find out how different it is from all other books. If we approach it with a kind of awed fear, if we open it as if it were a book of Magic, we miss both its human color and its divine message. It does not need the support of any theory of inspiration or authority: it is its own inspiration and speaks with its own authority—as we well know from the echo which it evokes in our hearts of the true and the good.

When a man reads the Bible as a Mason, he finds much to interest, surprise and delight, but he also misses much which he may have expected to find. To explain this paradox is one purpose of this chapter. He will discover, of course, in all its pages, even in the awful questioning of Job and the bitter pessimism of Ecclesiastes, the inescapable Belief in God which underlies and transfigures all its story. It is the one supreme book of faith in God, differing from other histories and literature not, in the facts which it records, but in its interpretation of the facts of life in the light of God. Also, the Mason will see with a new vividness and splendor those moral laws and principles which are in our human world like the great rock ribs which hold the earth together, and without which our human order would fall to pieces—or, in the words of Jesus, rot like meat without salt.

But the Mason, as he reads his Bible, will also find many things familiar to him in Masonry, in imagery as well as in idea, aside from its fundamental spiritual faith and moral command. The Bible is a chamber of imagery, a book of parables, a literature of symbols, and it shows us life under many metaphors, many similitudes, among them the imagery of architecture—man the builder, God the Builder, and men as living stones to be cut, polished, and built into a House of the Eternal; and we learn in a new setting the old symbolism of the working tools as we are taught to use them in the Lodge. A few examples will illustrate:

"Every house is builded by some man; but the builder of all things is God, whose house we are." Heb.3:4.

"Behold, I lay in Zion for a foundation a tried stone, a precious corner stone, a sure foundation." Isa. 28: 16.

"The stone which the builders rejected is become the head of the corner." Psa.108:22. Matt. 21:42.

"Ye also, as living stones, are built into a spiritual house." I. Pet. 2:5.

"When he set his compass upon the face of the deep, when he marked out the foundation of the earth: then was I by him as a master-workman." Provo 8:27-30.

"The Lord stood upon the wall made by a plumb line, with a plumb-line in his hand. Then said the Lord: Behold I will set a plumb-line in the midst of my people." Amos 7:7,8.

II

Yet the Mason will search the Bible in vain for anything, akin to a Masonic ceremony or degree. Even in the history of the building of the Temple by King Solomon-about which, the symbolism of the Craft in our day is woven-there is nothing which resembles, or even remotely suggests, what we are shown in the Lodge. To cite but one example: the tragedy of Hiram Abiff, so central in the mysteries of Masonry, is not met with even by hint or intimation in the Biblical record. Whether the people of the Bible had an esoteric teaching, or

THE GREAT LIGHT

an order of initiation, we do not know. If they did not, they were in this respect unlike almost all other peoples of the ancient world. If they did, they kept their secret so well that we have failed to find it out to this day.

How can we explain such a thing? Plainly by the fact that the Biblical coloring in Masonry—its scenery and setting—did not come into it directly from the Bible, but from secondary sources and by long, round-about ways which we are unable accurately to trace; so that by the time the Craft had taken its legendary, to say nothing of its ceremonial form, its dramas suggested by incidents in the Bible had been transformed into new shapes and put to new uses. The Legend of the Lost Word, the Substitute Word, the Great Temple, the Master Builder, all these, and much else in Masonry, no doubt had their original inspiration and suggestion directly from the Biblical narratives; but they have since traveled so far, passing through so many transformations, that they have well nigh lost all touch with their sources, and, as a fact, have become a system of universal symbolism, belonging equally to all men and all religions. And this is as we should like to have it, because Masonry, alike by its principles and its profession, is seeking to create a universal fellowship.

The drama of the Third Degree, as all agree, was modeled upon the drama of the Ancient Mysteries, a drama older than the Bible, older than the civilization whose origin and development the Bible records and interprets. When, where, and by whom this oldest of all dramas was taken up, recast, and given its Biblical setting and symbolism, nobody knows, and we may never learn. Some think it was the work of Jewish mystics in the Middle Ages-called Kabbalists - by whose influence and genius the Temple of King Solomon suddenly became, and remained for a long period, a center of symbolical thought, a focus of speculative philosophy. We do know that such was the fact, but whether it was due to the Kabbalists or not remains a mystery not yet solved. Anyway, out of the far past the wonder.ful thing we call Masonry emerged, making use of Biblical imagery and emblems, a teacher of wise and beautiful truth.

III

Let us now pass to matters more immediately practical, in order that the Mason may read his Bible to best advantage both to himself and to the Craft. Robert Louis Stevenson deemed it best to read the Bible by books, and there is much to be said for that method. For the Bible is not one book but many books—albeit a unity in its spirit and prophecy—each of its books having a time, a setting, and a message of its own. In order to understand any book of the Bible we must know, if possible, when it was written, where, by whom, and for what purpose, and here the whole world of scholarly research is ready and eager to help us. Let us take as an illustration the Book of Jonah, one of the most beautiful books in the world. The Book of Jonah was written, as nearly as we can determine, about 300 B.C., whereas the prophet Jonah, of whom it tells, lived in the reign of Jeroboam several hundred years earlier. Thus the author wrote after the events, seeking to interpret to his nation a series of tragic happenings which they did not understand—as a prophet today might seek to interpret to us the meaning of the Great War—and from which, apparently, they had learned nothing. Jonah was a real character and an ardent nationalist, but in the book he is used as a symbol of the nation, the spokesman of a narrow, bigoted imperialism, the better to show the tragedy of a narrow nationalism in conflict with the spiritual mission of the nation, in defiance of the large purpose of God to whom all nations are dear, and whose eternal good will embraces all mankind.

The Great Light

When we glance at the world situation of that time the meaning of the book becomes luminous. Two great empires, Assyria and Egypt, ruled the world, and their interests were in conflict. Assyria wanted an outlet on the Mediterranean Sea, much as Russia has long sought an outlet on a southern sea. Egypt opposed the ambitions of Assyria, dreading the competitions of commerce. Hence the sea and the storm in the book. Like Belgium between England and Germany, the little Hebrew nation lay between these two rival empires, their highway of trade in peace and a battleground in war. Egypt offered to make an alliance, and the Hebrew kings were in favor of it. But the prophets opposed it, denouncing it as an alliance with death and a covenant with hell. For, they argued, when the clash comes - when the storm of war breaks-and Egypt is hard pressed, she will throw the Hebrew nation overboard, and it will be swallowed by the Assyrian whale — a name by which more than one prophet described the Assyrian empire.

Anyway, the alliance was made in spite of the prophets. In due time the war came--shaking the earth as a storm shakes the sea—and Egypt, in sore straits, abandoned Israel, which was swallowed by the Assyrian whale and carried away into captivity. Later, after seventy years of exile, they were brought back to their native land, as Jonah was thrown up by the big fish on his own shores. Though the faith of the people was grandly steadfast through it all, they did not understand their ordeal, and this the prophet seeks to interpret in his book. Against this background, and read in this context, the book is a masterpiece in its literary art and its prophetic vision, showing us a new revelation of the nature and love of God, as much in its playful humor, its touches of tender irony, and its heart-breaking pathos, as in its sublime conception of history.

Jonah did not want to preach to Nineveh; he hated the city as a prophet of Belgium might hate Berlin—and he ran in the other direction. Nevertheless he had to go to Nineveh, and when he preached the whole city repented, from the king down to the beggar in the street. That is to say, Jonah saw his enemies forgiven and his hate defeated, and he was angry and prayed to die. With a touch of tender, ironic humor God answered his prayer—one can almost see Him pat the prophet on the head, as He replies: "Art thou so very angry?" Like a father trying to tease a naughty child out of a sulky mood, God made a gourd vine to grow over the booth and cover Jonah from the blazing sun. Jonah was glad; but the next day a worm bit the vine and it withered, and Jonah said: "It is better for me to die than to live." Then in one shining sentence the surly annoyance of Jonah at the withering of a gourd vine is set over against the infinite love and pity of God for a great city. It is a vision to break the heart, and mend it—revealing, in a blinding flash, the fathomless pity of God, His compassion for all peoples in all lands, yes, and even for the beasts that serve our need:

And the Lord said, Thou hast pity on the gourd, for which thou hast not labored, neither madest it to grow; which came up in a night and perished in a night; and should I not have pity on Nineveh, that great city; wherein are more than six score thousand persons that cannot discern between their right hand and their left (that is, little children); and also much cattle?"

IV

Thus, if we read the Bible aright, with insight and intelligence, it will melt our little bigotries and hatreds away, and make us tall of soul and tender of heart, Masters and Fellows of a wider Brotherhood. A word may be added about the different translations of the Bible, of which there are many in our day. For stately and musical English no version can rival the King James translation, whose rich antique diction is entwined with the holiest memories of our hearts, in whose very cadences we hear the echoes of voices now hushed. Yet some of the newer translations, by virtue of more recent researches,. are often more accurate; and they are printed in more attractive form, avoiding the "dim and crowded gray pages" of the older format. Here again a single example may illustrate how great a difference a little change of translation makes.

Take the old version of the words of Jesus in the Gospel of Luke: "In your patience possess ye your souls." The Revised Version of 1881 restored this text to its original force: "In your patience ye shall win your souls." One is tempted to say that all the work of the revisors was well spent had the only result been to secure this slight change, which lifts the words out of the commonplace into something rich and wonderful. For, slight as the change may seem, it marks the difference and distance between the soul as a treasure to be kept and a trophy to be won; between life as a possession and life as an adventure. That is to say, Jesus did not mean that his religion is a soft, cushioned faith, a refuge for the timid, a shelter of frail and delicate things, but a challenge to the heroic spirit, a quest and. conquest to stir the blood; a risk, a wager, a Divine foolishness; not a stick of candy but a stroke of lightning: "By your heroic patience ye shall purchase your souls!"

The Final Version of the Bible—better than King James, Moffatt, Goodspeed, or any other — the infinitely slower and more difficult translation of its truth into character, what a great soldier described as "an edition of the Bible bound in boot-leather," is among the things to be awaited. Alas, the Grand Style is as rare in life as it is in literature, and we shall have to wait much longer before we know how the Bible will read when it is translated into the lives of men and nations. Only a few words — here a line and there a stanza — have been wrought into action. For such a task we shall need to return again and again , for cleansing, for comfort, for command, to "the book of white samite, mystical and wonderful," where the sweet Voice is heard and the Vision dwells.